Welcome to your journal.

This journal is designed to help you reflect upon Scripture as you apply God's truth to your life.

It is a companion volume to t -
ing the Psalms to End your Wo
book *Living Without Fear: Usin*
and Anxiety Workbook.

As you read the book, and study the Psalms using the workbook, this journal provides you space for your own reflections and prayers.

Each page provides an inspiring quote from the Psalms, with room for you to write your ideas. A few select psalms are quoted in full to inspire you.

I pray that your life may be transformed as God's word moves deeply into your heart by his Spirit.

Kirsten Birkett

ISBN 978-1-7396907-3-1
Bible verses from World English Bible, public domain.

Blessed are all those who take refuge in him.
Psalm 2:12

You, Yahweh, are a shield around me,
my glory, and the one who lifts up my head.
Psalm 3:3

I cry to Yahweh with my voice
and he answers me out of his holy hill.
Psalm 3:4

I laid myself down and slept.
I awakened, for Yahweh sustains me.
Psalm 3:5

I will not be afraid of tens
of thousands of people
who have set themselves
against me on every side.
Psalm 3:6

Salvation belongs to Yahweh.
May your blessing be on
your people.
Psalm 3:8

Give me relief from my distress.
Have mercy on me, and hear my prayer.
Psalm 4:1

Yahweh will hear when I call to him. Psalm 4:3

You have put gladness in my heart,
more than when their grain and their new wine are increased.
Psalm 4:7

In peace I will both lay myself down and sleep,
for you alone, Yahweh, make me live in safety.
Psalm 4:8

In the abundance of your loving kindness I will come into your house.
Psalm 5:7

But let all those who take refuge in you rejoice.
Let them always shout for joy, because you defend them.
Psalm 5:11

Let them also who love your name be joyful in you.
Psalm 5:11

Yahweh has heard my supplication.
Yahweh accepts my prayer.
Psalm 6:9

I will give thanks to Yahweh
according to his righteousness,
and will sing praise to the name
of Yahweh Most High.
Psalm 7:17

Yahweh, our Lord, how majestic is your name in all the earth!
You have set your glory above the heavens!
Psalm 8:1

When I consider your heavens,
the work of your fingers,
the moon and the stars, which you have ordained,
what is man, that you think of him?
What is the son of man, that you care for him?
Psalm 8: 3-4

I will give thanks to Yahweh with my whole heart.
I will tell of all your marvelous works.
I will be glad and rejoice in you.
I will sing praise to your name,
O Most High.

Psalm 9:1-2

But Yahweh reigns forever.
He has prepared his throne for judgment.
He will judge the world in righteousness.
He will administer judgment to the peoples in uprightness.
Psalm 9:7-8

Those who know your name will put their trust in you,
for you, Yahweh, have not forsaken those who seek you.

Psalm 9:10

Arise, Yahweh!
God, lift up your hand!
Don't forget the helpless.

Psalm 10:12

Yahweh, you have heard the desire of the humble.

Psalm 10:17

For Yahweh is righteous.
He loves righteousness.
The upright shall see his face.
Psalm 11:7

Yahweh's words are ***flawless words,***
as silver refined in a clay furnace, purified seven times.
Psalm 12:6

But I trust in your loving kindness.
My heart rejoices in your salvation.
Psalm 13:5

I will sing to Yahweh,

because he has been good to me.

Psalm 13:6

I will bless Yahweh, who has given me counsel.
Yes, my heart instructs me in the night seasons.
Psalm 16:7

I have set Yahweh always before me.
Because he is at my right hand, I shall not be moved.
Psalm 16:8

You will show me the path of life.

In your presence is fullness of joy.

In your right hand there are pleasures forever more.

Psalm 16:11

Keep me as the apple of your eye.
Hide me under the shadow of your wings
Psalm 17:8

I love you, Yahweh, my strength.
Psalm 18:1

As for God, his way is perfect.
Yahweh's word is tried.
He is a shield to all those who take refuge in him.
Psalm 18:30

Yahweh lives! Blessed be my rock.
Exalted be the God of my salvation,
Psalm 18:46

The heavens declare the glory of God.
The expanse shows his handiwork.
Day after day they pour out speech,
and night after night they display knowledge.
There is no speech nor language
where their voice is not heard.
Their voice has gone out through all the earth,
their words to the end of the world.
Psalm 19:1-4

Yahweh's law is perfect, restoring the soul.
Yahweh's covenant is sure, making wise the simple.
Psalm 19:7

Yahweh's precepts are right, rejoicing the heart.
Yahweh's commandment is pure, enlightening the eyes.
Psalm 19:8-10

Let the words of my mouth and the meditation of my heart
be acceptable in your sight,
Yahweh, my rock, and my redeemer.
Psalm 19:14

May he grant you your heart's desire,
and fulfill all your counsel.
Psalm 20:4

Be *exalted*, Yahweh, in your strength,
so we will *sing* and *praise* your power.

Psalm 21:13

Don't be far from me, for trouble is near.
For there is no one to help.
Psalm 22:11

I will declare your name to my brothers.
Among the assembly, I will praise you.
Psalm 22:22

Psalm 23

A Psalm by David.

Yahweh is my shepherd;
I shall lack nothing.
He makes me lie down in green pastures.
He leads me beside still waters.
He restores my soul.
He guides me in the paths of righteousness for his name's sake.
Even though I walk through the valley of the shadow of death,
I will fear no evil, for you are with me.
Your rod and your staff,
they comfort me.
You prepare a table before me
in the presence of my enemies.
You anoint my head with oil.
My cup runs over.
Surely goodness and loving kindness shall follow me all the days of my life,
and I will dwell in Yahweh's house forever.

The earth is Yahweh's, with its fullness;
the world, and those who dwell in it.
Psalm 24:1

All the paths of Yahweh are loving kindness and truth
to such as keep his covenant and his testimonies.
Psalm 25:10

Yahweh is my light and my salvation.
Whom shall I fear?
Yahweh is the strength of my life.
Of whom shall I be afraid?
Psalm 27:1

Wait for Yahweh.
Be strong, and let your heart take courage.

Psalm 27:14

Yahweh is my strength and my shield.
My heart has trusted in him, and I am helped.
Therefore my heart greatly rejoices.
With my song I will thank him.
Psalm 28:7

Yahweh's voice is powerful.
Yahweh's voice is full of majesty.

Psalm 29:4

You have turned my mourning into dancing for me.
You have removed my sackcloth, and clothed me with gladness,
to the end that my heart may sing praise to you,
and not be silent.
Psalm 30:11-12

Praise be to Yahweh,
for he has shown me his marvelous loving kindness.
Psalm 31:21

Be glad in Yahweh, and rejoice, you righteous!
Shout for joy, all you who are upright in heart!
Psalm 32:11

For our heart rejoices in him,
because we have trusted in his holy name.
Let your loving kindness be on us, Yahweh,
since we have hoped in you.
Psalm 33:20-22

Oh *taste* and *see* that Yahweh is good.
Blessed is the man who takes refuge in him.
Psalm 34:8

The righteous cry, and Yahweh hears,
and delivers them out of all their troubles.
Psalm 34:17

Yahweh is near to those who have a broken heart,
and saves those who have a crushed spirit.
Psalm 34:18

Your loving kindness, Yahweh, is in the heavens.
Your faithfulness reaches to the skies.
Psalm 36:5

Also delight yourself in Yahweh,
and he will give you the desires of your heart.
Psalm 37:4

*Rest in Yahweh, and wait patiently for him.
Don't fret because of him who prospers in his way,
because of the man who makes wicked plots happen.*
Psalm 37:7

But the salvation of the righteous is from Yahweh.
He is their stronghold in the time of trouble.
Psalm 37:39

Blessed is he who considers the poor.
Yahweh will deliver him in the day of evil.
Psalm 41:1

My soul thirsts for God, for the living God.
When shall I come and appear before God?
Psalm 42:2

Why are you in despair, my soul?
Why are you disturbed within me?
Hope in God!
Psalm 42:5

Yahweh will command his loving kindness in the daytime.
In the night his song shall be with me: a prayer to the God of my life.
Psalm 42:8

God is our refuge and strength, a very present help in trouble.
Therefore we won't be afraid,
though the earth changes,
though the mountains are shaken into the heart of the seas.
Psalm 46:1-2

Shout to God with the voice of triumph!
For Yahweh Most High is awesome.
He is a great King over all the earth.
Psalm 47:1-2

Sing praises to God! Sing praises!
Sing praises to our King!
Sing praises!
Psalm 47:6

Purify me with hyssop, and I will be clean.
Wash me, and I will be whiter than snow.
Let me hear joy and gladness,
that the bones which you have broken may rejoice.
Psalm 51:7-8

Restore to me the joy of your salvation.
Uphold me with a willing spirit.
Psalm 51:12

I *trust*
in God*'s*
loving kindness
forever and ever.
P*salm* 52:8

I will give you thanks forever,
because you have done it.
I will hope in your name, for it is good,
in the presence of your saints.
Psalm 52:9

I will give thanks to your name, Yahweh,
for it is good.
Psalm 54:6

I said, "Oh that I had wings like a dove!
Then I would fly away, and be at rest."
Psalm 55:6

Cast your burden on Yahweh and he will sustain you.
He will never allow the righteous to be moved.
Psalm 55:22

I *will trust in you.*
Psalm 55:23

When I am afraid,

I will put my trust in you.

Psalm 56:3

I know this:

that God is for me.

In God, I will praise his word.

In Yahweh, I will praise his word.

Psalm 56: 9-10

I have put my trust in God.
I will not be afraid.
What can man do to me?
Psalm 56:11

My heart is steadfast, God.
My heart is steadfast.
I will sing, yes, I will sing praises.
Psalm 57:7

Oh, my Strength, I watch for you,
for God is my high tower.
My God will go before me with his loving kindness.
Psalm 59:9-10

But I will sing of your strength.
Yes, I will sing aloud of your loving kindness in the morning.
Psalm 59:16

My soul rests in God alone.
My salvation is from him.
He alone is my rock, my salvation, and my fortress.
I will never be greatly shaken.
Psalm 62:1-2

My soul, wait in silence for God alone,
for my expectation is from him.
Psalm 62:5

God has spoken once;
twice I have heard this,
that power belongs to God.
Also to you, Lord, belongs loving kindness
Psalm 62:11-12

*God, you are my God.
I will earnestly seek you.
My soul thirsts for you.*
Psalm 63:1

Because your loving kindness is better than life,
my lips shall praise you.
So I will bless you while I live.
I will lift up my hands in your name.
Psalm 63:3-4

The righteous shall be glad in Yahweh, and shall take refuge in him.
All the upright in heart shall praise him!

Psalm 64:9-10

Sins overwhelmed me,
but you atoned for our transgressions.
Blessed is the one whom you choose and cause to come near,
that he may live in your courts.
We will be filled with the goodness of your house,
your holy temple.
Psalm 65:3-4

You call the morning's dawn and the evening with songs of joy.
Psalm 65:8

You visit the earth, and water it.
You greatly enrich it.
The river of God is full of water.
You provide them grain, for so you have ordained it.
Psalm 65:9

Make a joyful shout to God, all the earth!
Sing to the glory of his name!
Offer glory and praise!
Psalm 66:1

All the earth will worship you,
and will sing to you;
they will sing to your name."
Psalm 66:4

Come, and see God's deeds—
awesome work on behalf of the children of men.
Psalm 66:5

Praise our God, you peoples!
Make the sound of his praise heard,
Psalm 66:8

Blessed be God, who has not turned away my prayer,
nor his loving kindness from me.
Psalm 66:20

May God be merciful to us, bless us,
and cause his face to shine on us.
Psalm 67:1

Oh let the nations be glad and sing for joy,
for you will judge the peoples with equity,
and govern the nations on earth.
Psalm 67:4

But let the righteous be glad.
Let them rejoice before God.
Yes, let them rejoice with gladness.
Psalm 68:3

A father of the fatherless, and a defender of the widows,
is God in his holy habitation.
God sets the lonely in families.
He brings out the prisoners with singing,
Psalm 68:5-6

Blessed be the Lord, who daily bears our burdens,
even the God who is our salvation.
Psalm 68:19

God is to us a God of deliverance.
To Yahweh, the Lord, belongs escape from death.
Psalm 68:20

Answer me, Yahweh, for your loving kindness is good.
According to the multitude of your tender mercies, turn to me.
Don't hide your face from your servant,
for I am in distress.
Answer me speedily!
Psalm 69:16-17

But I am in pain and distress.
Let your salvation, God, protect me.
Psalm 69:29

I will praise the name of God with a song,
and will magnify him with thanksgiving.
Psalm 69:30

The humble have seen it, and are glad.
You who seek after God, let your heart live.
Psalm 69:32

Hurry, God, to deliver me.
Come quickly to help me, Yahweh.
Psalm 70:1

*Let all those who seek you rejoice and be glad in you.
Let those who love your salvation continually say,
"Let God be exalted!"*
Psalm 70:4

In you, Yahweh, I take refuge.
Never let me be disappointed.
Psalm 71:1

My mouth shall be filled with your praise,
with your honor all day long.
Psalm 71:8

Don't reject me in my old age.
Don't forsake me when my strength fails.
Psalm 71:9

God, don't be far from me.
My God, hurry to help me.
Psalm 71:12

But I will always hope,
and will add to all of your praise.
Psalm 71:14

Yes, even when I am old and gray-haired, God, don't forsake me,
until I have declared your strength to the next generation,
your might to everyone who is to come.
Psalm 71:18

Praise be to Yahweh God, the God of Israel,
who alone does marvelous deeds.
Blessed be his glorious name forever!
Let the whole earth be filled with his glory!
Amen and amen.
Psalm 72:18-19

Whom do I have in heaven?
There is no one on earth whom I desire besides you.
Psalm 73:25

The day is yours, the night is also yours.
You have prepared the light and the sun.
You have set all the boundaries of the earth.
You have made summer and winter.
Psalm 74:16-17

We give thanks to you, God.
We give thanks, for your Name is near.
Men tell about your wondrous works.
Psalm 75:1

I will also meditate on all your work,
and consider your doings.
Psalm 77:12

Cause your face to shine,
and we will be saved.
Psalm 80:3

Sing aloud to God, our strength!
Make a joyful shout to the God of Jacob!
Psalm 81:1

Raise a song, and bring here the tambourine,
the pleasant lyre with the harp.
Psalm 81:2

My soul longs, and even faints for the courts of Yahweh.
My heart and my flesh cry out for the living God.
Psalm 84:2

Blessed is the man who trusts in you.
Psalm 84:12

Yahweh, you have been favorable to your land.
You have restored the fortunes of Jacob.
You have forgiven the iniquity of your people.
You have covered all their sin.
Psalm 85:1

Won't you revive us again,
that your people may rejoice in you?
Psalm 85:6

Show us your loving kindness, Yahweh.
Grant us your salvation.
Psalm 85:7

Mercy and truth meet together.
Righteousness and peace have kissed each other.
Psalm 85:10

Bring joy to the soul of your servant,
for to you, Lord, do I lift up my soul.
Psalm 86:4

For you, Lord, are good, and ready to forgive,
abundant in loving kindness to all those who call on you.
Psalm 86:5

Hear, Yahweh, my prayer.
Listen to the voice of my petitions.
Psalm 86:6

In the day of my trouble I will call on you,
for you will answer me.
Psalm 86:7

There is no one like you among the gods, Lord,
nor any deeds like your deeds.
All nations you have made will come and worship before you, Lord.
They shall glorify your name.
For you are great, and do wondrous things.
You are God alone.

Psalm 86:7-10

Teach me your way, Yahweh.
I will walk in your truth.
Psalm 86:11

I will praise you, Lord my God, with my whole heart.
I will glorify your name forever more.
Psalm 86:12

Yahweh, the God of my salvation,
I have cried day and night before you.
Let my prayer enter into your presence.
Turn your ear to my cry.
For my soul is full of troubles.
Psalm 88:1-3

I will sing of the loving kindness of Yahweh forever.
With my mouth, I will make known your faithfulness
to all generations.
Psalm 89:1

Blessed be Yahweh forever more.
Amen, and Amen.
Psalm 89:52

Before the mountains were born,
before you had formed the earth and the world,
even from everlasting to everlasting,

you are God.

Psalm 90:2

So teach us to count our days,
that we may gain a heart of wisdom.
Psalm 90:12

Satisfy us in the morning with your loving kindness,
that we may rejoice and be glad all our days.
Psalm 90:14

I will say of Yahweh, "He is my refuge and my fortress;
my God, in whom I trust."
Psalm 91:2

It is a good thing to give thanks to Yahweh,
to sing praises to your name, Most High,
to proclaim your loving kindness in the morning,
and your faithfulness every night,
with the ten-stringed lute, with the harp,
and with the melody of the lyre.
Psalm 92:1-3

For you, Yahweh, have made me glad through your work.
I will triumph in the works of your hands.
Psalm 92:4

How great are your works, Yahweh!
Your thoughts are very deep.
Psalm 92:5

The righteous shall flourish like the palm tree.
He will grow like a cedar in Lebanon.
Psalm 92:12

Your statutes stand firm.
Holiness adorns your house,
Yahweh, forever more.
Psalm 93:5

When I said, "My foot is slipping!"
Your loving kindness, Yahweh, held me up.
In the multitude of my thoughts within me,
your comforts delight my soul.

Psalm 94:18-19

Oh come, let's sing to Yahweh.
Let's shout aloud to the rock of our salvation!
Let's come before his presence with thanksgiving.
Let's extol him with songs!
Psalm 95:1-2

For Yahweh is a great God,
a great King above all gods.
Psalm 95:3

Oh come, let's worship and bow down.
Let's kneel before Yahweh, our Maker,
for he is our God.
We are the people of his pasture,
and the sheep in his care.
Psalm 95:6-7

Sing to Yahweh a new song!
Sing to Yahweh, all the earth.
Psalm 96:1

Let the heavens be glad, and let the earth rejoice.
Let the sea roar, and its fullness!
Let the field and all that is in it exult!
Then all the trees of the woods shall sing for joy
before Yahweh;
Psalm 96:11-12

Yahweh reigns!
Let the earth rejoice!
Let the multitude of islands be glad!
Psalm 97:1

The heavens declare his righteousness.
All the peoples have seen his glory.
Psalm 97:6

Light is sown for the righteous,
and gladness for the upright in heart.
Psalm 97:11

Make a joyful noise to Yahweh, all the earth!
Burst out and sing for joy, yes, sing praises!
Sing praises to Yahweh with the harp,
with the harp and the voice of melody.
With trumpets and sound of the ram's horn,
make a joyful noise before the King, Yahweh.

Psalm 98:4-6

Let the mountains sing for joy together.
Let them sing before Yahweh
Psalm 98:8-9

Exalt Yahweh our God.
Worship at his footstool.
He is Holy!
Psalm 99:5

Exalt Yahweh, our God.
Worship at his holy hill,
for Yahweh, our God, is holy!
Psalm 99:9

Psalm 100

A Psalm of thanksgiving.

Shout for joy to Yahweh, all you lands!
Serve Yahweh with gladness.
Come before his presence with singing.
Know that Yahweh, he is God.
It is he who has made us, and we are his.

We are his people,
and the sheep of his pasture.
Enter into his gates with thanksgiving,
and into his courts with praise.
Give thanks to him, and bless his name.

For Yahweh is good.
His loving kindness endures forever,
his faithfulness to all generations.

I will sing of loving kindness and justice.
To you, Yahweh, I will sing praises.
Psalm 101:1

Praise Yahweh, my soul!
All that is within me, praise his holy name!
Psalm 103:1

who satisfies your desire with good things,
so that your youth is renewed like the eagle's.
Psalm 103:5

Yahweh is merciful and gracious,
slow to anger, and abundant in loving kindness
Psalm 103:8

For as the heavens are high above the earth,
so great is his loving kindness toward those who fear him.
Psalm 103:11

Bless Yahweh, my soul.
Yahweh, my God, you are very great.
You are clothed with honor and majesty.
Psalm 104:1

He sends springs into the valleys.
They run among the mountains.
They give drink to every animal of the field.
The wild donkeys quench their thirst.
The birds of the sky nest by them.
They sing among the branches.
Psalm 104:10-12

He appointed the moon for seasons.
The sun knows when to set
Psalm 104:19

Yahweh, how many are your works!
In wisdom, you have made them all.
The earth is full of your riches
Psalm 104:24

Let Yahweh's glory endure forever.
Let Yahweh rejoice in his works.
32 He looks at the earth, and it trembles.
He touches the mountains, and they smoke.
Psalm 104:31-32

I will sing to Yahweh as long as I live.
I will sing praise to my God while I have any being.
Let my meditation be sweet to him.
I will rejoice in Yahweh.

Psalm 104:33-34

Sing to him, sing praises to him!
Tell of all his marvelous works.
Psalm 105:2

Glory in his holy name.
Let the heart of those who seek Yahweh rejoice.
Psalm 105:3

He opened the rock, and waters gushed out.
They ran as a river in the dry places.
For he remembered his holy word,
and Abraham, his servant.
Psalm 105:41-42

He brought his people out with joy,
his chosen with singing.
Psalm 105:43

Give thanks to Yahweh, for he is good,
for his loving kindness endures forever.
Who can utter the mighty acts of Yahweh,
or fully declare all his praise?
Psalm 106:1-2

Blessed be Yahweh, the God of Israel,
from everlasting even to everlasting!
Let all the people say, "Amen."
Psalm 106:48

Give thanks to Yahweh,[*]

for he is good,

for his loving kindness endures forever.

Psalm 107:1

Let them offer the
sacrifices of thanksgiving,
and declare his deeds with singing.
Psalm 107:22

Whoever is wise will pay attention to these things.
They will consider the loving kindnesses of Yahweh
Psalm 107:43

My heart is steadfast, God.
I will sing and I will make music with my soul.
Wake up, harp and lyre!
For I am poor and needy.
My heart is wounded within me.

Psalm 109:22

Help me, Yahweh, my God.
Save me according to your loving kindness;
Psalm 109:26

Yahweh has sworn, and will not change his mind
Psalm 110:4

Yahweh's works are great,
pondered by all those who delight in them.
Psalm 111:2

The fear of Yahweh is the beginning of wisdom.
All those who do his work have a good understanding.
His praise endures forever!
Psalm 111:10

Blessed is the man who fears Yahweh,
who delights greatly in his commandments.
Psalm 112:1

From the rising of the sun to its going down,
Yahweh's name is to be praised.
Psalm 113:3

He raises up the poor out of the dust,
and lifts up the needy from the ash heap.
Psalm 113:7

Yahweh remembers us. He will bless us.
Psalm 115:12

I love Yahweh, because he listens to my voice,
and my cries for mercy.
Psalm 116:1

Because he has turned his ear to me,
therefore I will call on him
as long as I live.
Psalm 116:2
Yahweh preserves the simple.

I was brought low, and he saved me.
Psalm 116:6

Psalm 117

Praise Yahweh, all you nations!
Extol him, all you peoples!
For his loving kindness is
great toward us.
Yahweh's faithfulness
endures forever.
Praise Yah!

Yahweh is on my side. I will not be afraid.
What can man do to me?
Psalm 118:6

This is the day that Yahweh has made.
We will rejoice and be glad in it!
Psalm 118:24

I *rise before dawn and cry for help.*
I *put my hope in your words.*
P*salm* 119:147:

Praise him, sun and moon!
Praise him, all you shining stars!
Psalm 148:3

Psalm 150

Praise Yah!
Praise God in his sanctuary!
Praise him in his heavens for his acts of power!
Praise him for his mighty acts!
Praise him according to his excellent greatness!
Praise him with the sounding of the trumpet!
Praise him with harp and lyre!
Praise him with tambourine and dancing!
Praise him with stringed instruments and flute!
Praise him with loud cymbals!
Praise him with resounding cymbals!
Let everything that has breath praise Yah!
Praise Yah!

Printed in Dunstable, United Kingdom

70354131R00117